# Uncharted, Unexplored, and Unexplained

## Scientific Advancements of the 19th Century

# Joseph Lister

## and the Story of Antiseptics

*Mitchell Lane*
**PUBLISHERS**

P.O. Box 196
Hockessin, Delaware
19707

# Uncharted, Unexplored, and Unexplained

## Scientific Advancements of the 19th Century

## Titles in the Series

Visit us on the web: www.mitchelllane.com
Comments? email us: mitchelllane@mitchelllane.com

# Uncharted, Unexplored, and Unexplained

## Scientific Advancements of the 19th Century

# Joseph Lister
## and the Story of Antiseptics

by John Bankston

# Uncharted, Unexplored, and Unexplained

## Scientific Advancements of the 19th Century

*Mitchell Lane*
**PUBLISHERS**

Printing      1    2    3    4    5    6    7    8
        Library of Congress Cataloging-in-Publication Data
Bankston, John, 1974-
        Joseph Lister and the story of antiseptics / John Bankston.
             p. cm. — (Uncharted, unexplored & unexplained: scientific advancements of
        the 19th century)
Includes bibliographical references and index.
        ISBN 1-58415-262-1 (lib. bdg.)
        1.  Lister, Joseph, Baron, 1827-1912—Juvenile literature. 2. Surgeons—Great Britain—
Biography—Juvenile literature. 3.  Surgery, Aseptic and antiseptic—Juvenile literature.
[1. Lister, Joseph, Baron, 1827-1912. 2. Physicians. 3. Antiseptics. 4. Medicine—
History.]  I. Title. II. Uncharted, unexplored & unexplained.
        R489.L75B36 2005
        617'.092--dc22

        J617.092
        L773 B7
                                                              2003024132

**ABOUT THE AUTHOR:** Born in Boston, Massachussetts, **John Bankston** began publishing articles in newspapers and magazines while still a teenager. Since then, he has written over two hundred articles, and contributed chapters to books such as *Crimes of Passion,* and *Death Row 2000,* which have been sold in bookstores across the world. He has written numerous biographies for young adults, including *Jonas Salk and the Polio Vaccine* and *Alexander Fleming and the Story of Penicillin* (Mitchell Lane). He currently lives in Portland, Oregon.

# Uncharted, Unexplored, and Unexplained

## Scientific Advancements of the 19th Century

## Joseph Lister

### and the Story of Antiseptics

*For Your Information

James Young Simpson, shown here, was a Scottish physician and the discoverer of chloroform. As a professor of Midwifery at Edinburgh University, he was aware of his patients' suffering. In 1847, he tested chloroform, which was then used in childbirth for many years, until it was discovered to cause irreversible liver damage.

# 1

# Cause of Death

They built the hospital over a cemetery. Maybe *that's* why the patients were dying.

In 1861, the Royal Infirmary in Glasgow, Scotland, expanded. A new surgical wing was constructed—right over the graves of generations of dead bodies. With an extra 144 beds and a spanking new building, the administrators hoped they'd solved an age-old problem.

They hadn't.

Just a few years before, the discoverer of chloroform anesthesia, James Y. Simpson, wrote a pamphlet. In it he noted, "A man laid on the operating table in one of our surgical hospitals is exposed to more chances of death than was the English soldier on the field of Waterloo."[1]

Simpson gave a name to the condition he believed to be deadlier than the battlefield that marked the final defeat of Napoleon in 1815. He called it "hospitalism."

In the nineteenth century, surviving surgery was only half the battle. In many hospitals, 50 percent of amputees—people who had one or more of their arms or legs cut off—lived through their painful operations but died soon afterward in their beds. "Operation successful, patient died" was a common entry in nineteenth century medical records.

No one knew how to prevent hospitalism. Some suggested putting up new buildings, or even small "surgical huts." Yet the new wing at Glasgow did nothing to diminish the rate of death. Some people wondered if evil spirits were responsible. In 1843, a time when many people considered ghosts to be as real as the Royal Infirmary, Charles Dickens's bestseller *A Christmas Carol* described one ghost that could have sprung from the graveyard, "for in the very air through which the spirit moved, it seemed to scatter gloom and mystery. It was shrouded in a deep black garment which concealed its head, its face, its form and left nothing of it visible save one outstretched hand."[2]

Novels about haunted buildings weren't the reason one doctor worried that the dead were killing the living. The Glasgow hospital employees made a gruesome discovery in their basement. They unearthed bodies of cholera victims: men, women and children who'd died during an 1849 epidemic.

"A few inches below the surface of the ground," Joseph Lister wrote in a December, 1869, article in The *Lancet*, a highly respected British medical journal, "on a level with the floor of the two lowest male accident wards, with only the basement area, four feet wide intervening, was found the uppermost tier of coffins, which had been placed there at the time of the cholera epidemic of 1849, the corpses having undergone so little change... that the clothes they had on were [still visible.]"[3]

Cholera was a highly contagious disease that killed thousands of people, but doctors weren't sure how it was spread. Hoping to prevent a wave of hospitalism, they soaked the bodies in lime and acid. That liquefied the bodies, but hospitalism continued.

Joseph Lister had an idea. What if the spread of disease had nothing to do with the rotting bodies?

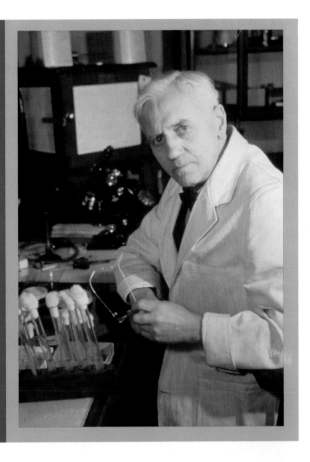

Alexander Fleming, shown here, was a Scottish bacteriologist. He worked at St. Mary's Hospital during and after World War I where he worked on developing a way to reduce the number of deaths from infection in soldiers. One day in 1928, before tossing some old petri dishes of culture away, he made an accidental discovery of blue mold growing on the culture of some harmful bacteria. The mold seemed to be able to kill the bacteria. His finding led to the discovery of penicillin.

Most famous men of medicine make discoveries that save lives. Some, such as untidy Alexander Fleming, find a new drug. He discovered penicillin, the first antibiotic. Others, like Jonas Salk, prevent a disease from spreading. His polio vaccine halted one of the most feared diseases of the twentieth century.

Joseph Lister's work didn't focus on a new drug or a specific disease. Although he was a surgeon, he isn't known for an innovative surgical technique. Though Lister did his work in the nineteenth century, it was so revolutionary that many of his practices are still used in the twenty-first. Whenever a surgeon snaps on a pair of rubber gloves or a dentist slips on a mask, it is largely because of this pioneer. His work is so important that surgical history is divided into two eras: "Before Lister" and "After Lister."

He began his training in hospitals that didn't change the sheets from one patient to the next, at a time when surgeons would finish one operation and embark on another one without washing their hands. Using a variety of techniques, some of which are still used today, Joseph pushed hospitals to clean up their acts. Yet at the time, many people thought he was a little nuts. An earlier doctor who'd recommended clean conditions wound up in an insane asylum. Joseph himself had had a nervous breakdown as a young adult.

It often takes the weight of numbers to change minds. Joseph's techniques reduced death rates by up to 60 percent. Before he died, he'd see hospitals where the sheets were changed, where surgeons washed their hands and wore gloves. His antiseptic methods changed surgery in both his lifetime and ours.

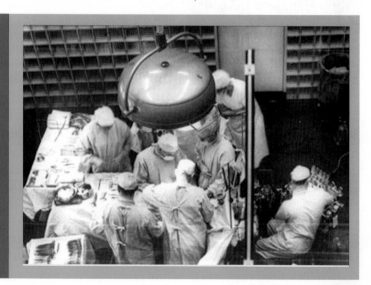

Today surgeons wear masks and gloves to protect patients from bacteria. It was Joseph Lister and his antiseptic methods that made surgery much safer.

Author *Charles Dickens in his enormously popular novels recorded many of the horrible living conditions that Joseph Lister witnessed. Dickens was the son of a Navy clerk who lost his money and wound up in debtors' prison when Charles was twelve. He had to go to work in a factory that made blacking for boots. Even though it lasted for only a few months, it was a terrible experience for the sensitive boy. One result was that Charles identified with the poor even as he grew rich. His sympathy for those who had little money was similar to Joseph Lister's.*

Charles Dickens

*After completing school, Charles became a clerk in the House of Commons in the English Parliament. Then he worked as a newspaper reporter, and began fashioning stories that appeared in local publications like* True Son *and* Mirror of Parliament. *In 1836 his books* The Pickwick Papers *and* Sketches by Boz *were popular enough that he could quit his job and devote his time to writing.*

*He wrote other famous books such as* Oliver Twist, David Copperfield, A Tale of Two Cities, Great Expectations *and* A Christmas Carol. *Since most of his stories were published in installments or serials in magazines, Dickens's fans had to wait for a new chapter every week or every month. People could hardly wait for the next installment to appear. In New York City, people lined up along the docks, waiting for the latest shipment to come across the Atlantic Ocean.*

*He added to his appeal by becoming a successful public speaker, reading from his works. He used his prominent position to advocate for issues such as ending slavery.*

*Until his death in 1870, the public eagerly awaited the next Dickens story. His classic works continue to be widely read. They have also been seen in numerous film versions and on stage.*

An archival illustration depicting a Quaker meeting in France in the mid-1700s. Joseph Lister's father, Joseph Jackson Lister, was a leader in the Society of Friends. His family had been members of the church for generations.

# 2

# Friendly Persuasions

Joseph Lister wasn't the first person in his family to make an earth-shattering scientific discovery. His father, Joseph Jackson Lister, did his part to advance medical knowledge, and he never even graduated from high school.

Although Joseph Jackson left school at fourteen to join his father's wine business, he was hardly a typical dropout. He continued to study advanced mathematics. He read classic literature in its original Latin, and spoke both German and French. At eighteen he became a full partner in the company. It included warehouses, wine cellars and even a ship used to take the products from the company's home base in England to continental Europe.

Being so successful at a young age wasn't enough for Joseph Jackson. He also became a leader in the Society of Friends, or Quakers as they are more commonly known. His family had been members of the church for generations. He carefully followed its teachings, which emphasized good works and personal achievement.

Joseph Jackson did both by combining math and science to help mankind. In 1824, he began applying mathematical formulas to crafting lenses for microscopes. Although widely used in the early 1800s, micro-

An early microscope designed by Robert Hooke. Lister's father, Joseph Jackson Lister, ground his own lenses and improved the quality of the microscope. Manufacturers copied his idea.

scopes were plagued by problems. As people looked at slides in the proper white light, the lens sometimes acted as a prism, producing a rainbow effect. At high levels of magnification, the image became blurry. Joseph Jackson ground his own lenses and greatly improved their quality.

By writing scientific papers with his friend Dr. Thomas Hodgkin (who discovered the form of lymphatic cancer that bears his name), Joseph Jackson began developing a reputation in medical circles. His 1830 paper published in the Royal Society of London's publication, *Philosophical Translations,* dramatically improved laboratory research. In it, he detailed his work with microscopes and included the specifications for the lenses he designed. Soon manufacturers copied his ideas. Although the design didn't make him rich, the science of bacteriology would not have emerged without the improvement in lens magnification he devised. It was this discipline that would have a profound influence on Joseph Jackson's second son, who was born only a few years before the publication of his father's noteworthy paper.

Joseph Jackson and his wife, Isabella, already had three children—Mary, John and Isabella Sophie—when Joseph Lister was born. Isabella gave birth to the couple's second son on April 27, 1827 at the family home in Upton Park, a nearly seventy-acre estate just east of London. Growing up, young Joseph had woods to play in and plenty of animals to play with. The Listers kept everything from rabbits and chickens to cows and even a deer, and they treated them more like pets than future meals.

Joseph's father had bought the century-old home just a year before; by the time Joseph was a toddler his father was teaching him how to read and write. The house held a collection of the family's interests, which ranged from expensively bound books to the fossils that took up so much space the first floor was nicknamed "The Museum." No matter how many shelves they consumed, books were always popular gifts among the family members. For his sixth birthday, Joseph received *Evenings at Home*, a collection of fables, stories and natural history. Like the rest of the Lister children, Joseph began reading the Bible at a young age; he regularly got new editions as presents.

The family home was a good place for the future man of medicine to receive an early education. He often watched his father with his scientific studies and asked questions. His writing ability blossomed early, as a letter written to his aunt in 1833 reflects: "I am very much pleased to write thee a letter and to tell thee bout our bees. Thomas Nutt came here yesterday and brought a hive of bees into the dining-room and put a sort of lantern with some sack in the paper into a green bag by the hive, hung over it which made the bees tipsy."[1]

The Lister family continued to grow with the addition of William Henry, Arthur and Jane. Most families were close in the early 1800s, with children settling near their parents when they grew up. Yet the Listers were unusual even for their time, as several eventually bought property within walking distance of the family estate, and all relied on their family's support well into adulthood.

Among all the children, few needed as much extra attention as Joseph. Fortunately his parents were willing to give it.

Joseph had a speech impediment. Whenever he was excited or nervous, he stuttered severely—making him impossible to understand. In the 1830s, it wasn't exactly the worst problem a kid could have. Still, it was bad enough that his father decided to home-school him, an unusual choice for a middle class British family in the 1800s.

Joseph's father tutored him in math, English, Latin and of course science. He also worked on his stutter. By the time he was eleven he was strong enough academically to be accepted to The Hitchin School. Sister Mary wrote brother John, "He says he does not stammer at all, and the boys do not even know that he does so as Master did not tell anyone."[2]

The Quakers ran the Hitchin School. Located in Hertfordshire, along the rail line between Birmingham and London, it was a popular choice for Quaker families. The train made it possible for Joseph's family to make regular visits. It was also the first step towards modern transportation, which would eventually absorb Upton Park into East London.

Before he turned fourteen, he'd advanced enough academically to attend Grove House, a Quaker high school in Tottenham. He became very involved in the school's science program, and illustrated many of his projects with his own drawings. Some people believe that his interest in medicine may have begun at this time.

Two years later Lister's father decided his second son was ready for an even steeper challenge: college. Joseph would be the first in the family to go. Even with his father's financial help, Joseph faced obstacles.

The Quakers rejected any kind of church authority, including the Church of England. The most prestigious universities in England were Oxford and Cambridge. Both included religious tests as part of the entrance exam. As a Quaker, Joseph couldn't take them. Instead, he applied to a much newer and less respected school with fewer require-ments: University College, which was part of the University of London.

Once he was admitted, Joseph took a single course—botany. Study-ing plants and flowers, he assembled an impressive specimen collection that he kept for the rest of his life.

At the age of seventeen, he moved into an apartment. Alone in the big city of London and not having to work because his parents were paying both tuition and rent, Lister had more freedom than most kids his age could have imagined. Yet it seems he did little other than attend classes and church meetings. He hung out with John Hodgkin, the son of his father's science partner, and roommate Edward Palmer, who later remembered, "His friends always felt his power, but it was silently exerted power. He lived in the world of his thoughts, modest, unmasterful, unassuming..."[3]

There were reasons for this. He'd been raised in the quiet religion of the Quakers. His stutter forced him to speak slowly, emotionlessly. His thoughts became less quiet by the time he enrolled as a full time stu-dent. When he attended Quaker services he was seized by a need to speak out. Quakers held "silent meetings," which allowed the members to feel "God's presence." His friend Hodgkin would later recall Joseph's "outrageous" behavior: "I shall never forget the amazement and fear with which I saw him stand up in the silent meeting and utter the words, 'I will be with thee and keep thee! Fear thou not.'...At the time for so young a man to 'speak in meeting' was looked on as something awful."[4]

The rebellion was minor compared to what parents today expect from their teens. Yet it indicated a struggle, "a religious conflict of the soul," as Hodgkin put it. Speaking to the other members as he had indicated a possible interest in pursuing the ministry.

The year before, Joseph took just a single math class while contem-plating a career as an artist. In 1847, his direction changed after watch-ing professor of surgery Robert Liston's operations. Brought in by his

17

Robert Liston was a Scottish surgeon who was the professor of clinical surgery at University College in London from 1827 until his death in 1847. Joseph Lister changed his direction in life after watching one of Liston's operations.

friend Palmer, he witnessed the first surgery in England performed under ether, a type of anesthesia. Joseph began to contemplate a surgical career.

His parents, pleased their son wasn't going to waste time pursuing a frivolous career, were stunned when he considered becoming a minister instead. After graduating with a Bachelor of Arts degree in December 1847, the pressure must have been tremendous. Like many teens, Joseph was torn between what he wanted to do and what he *should* do.

As difficult as choosing his future was, Joseph was already suffering from more painful losses. In October 1846, his brother John had died. Although his death was most likely the result of a brain tumor, John also came down with smallpox shortly before his death. The next year Joseph suffered a mild form of the illness and may have felt he'd survived a brush with death. Since medical care could do nothing to save his brother, he may have questioned the point of going into medicine.

Regardless of the cause, the conflicts came to a head in March of 1848. He suffered a nervous breakdown, and plunged into a deep depression. Unable to work or study, he went home to Upton Park. Some accounts suggest he even thought about killing himself.

Ilfracombe from the Torrs.

An illustration of the beach resort Ilfracombe as it looked in 1850, around the time that Lister came to recover from a bout with depression.

Joseph Jackson worried about his son's future, but he worried about his health even more. He'd just endured the loss of another of his sons, and Isabella was sick during their entire marriage, most likely from a weak heart. Joseph Jackson was a compassionate husband.

He was a compassionate father as well. In June he paid for Edward Palmer to take Joseph to Ilfracombe, a beach resort. In a letter to his son, he wrote, "I do entertain a hopeful trust that this excursion may be permitted to be the means of restoring both thy bodily and mental powers."[5]

Palmer was a decent companion of the younger student, although he would later suffer from mental illness himself. Joseph healed slowly. He traveled to the Dublin, Ireland, home of a wealthy Quaker named Thomas Pim and spent time in Germany early the next year.

Finally the travel and rest did their work. Joseph recovered, though the breakdown's emotional scars never disappeared. He stopped drawing for pleasure. He kept his emotions bottled up, and soon earned a reputation as cold and distant. His few friendships became less close. But he also became more focused, as a surgical career became foremost in his mind.

In the fall of 1849, he registered as a medical student at University College. By August 1850, he'd placed second in examinations for Honors in Anatomy and Physiology. By the fall, the Medical Committee offered him an appointment as dresser. The job required that he work under the guidance of one of the two surgeons at University Hospital, interviewing patients, recording their case histories, assisting during operations and recording outcomes, including deaths. The position only went to the top students—an enormous honor for anyone selected.

Joseph turned it down. Maybe he didn't feel strong enough.

Three months later, he changed his mind. When he was again offered the dresser position, he took it. Joseph Lister was about to witness the horrors of hospitalism first-hand.

Quakers are members of the Society of Friends, a religious order begun in the seventeenth century by George Fox. Fox, who was born in 1624, believed that the Catholic and Anglican churches represented a barrier between the congregation and God.

Fox had the vision that began his new religion in May 1652, as he climbed Pendle Hill in England. "As we traveled we came near a very great hill," he wrote in his autobiography, "and I was moved of the Lord to go up to the very top of it; which I did with difficulty, it was so very steep and high...From the top of the hill the Lord let me see in what places he had a great people to be gathered."⁶ Believing that the Lord had moved him to begin the Society of Friends, Fox spoke of his vision to the inn-keeper where he spent that night and soon to many others.

William Penn

He proposed a new church, where everyone was equal and the individual's personal relationship with God was the most important. Members became known as Quakers because they would often tremble or "quake" when they felt they were communicating directly with God. The religion treated men and women as equals, and while it had ministers, they weren't the powerful priests who existed in the 1600s. Instead, everyone had a voice in the direction of the church.

While his message attracted many supporters, he angered the religious establishment. Fox and other Quakers were often arrested. By some estimates, Fox spent a total of more than six years in prison.

In the late 1600s, many Quakers left the religious persecution they faced in England and came to the New World. One of them, William Penn, founded what would become the future state of Pennsylvania.

English nursing reformer Florence Nightingale was the first woman to receive the Order of Merit for her tireless efforts during the Crimean War.

# 3

# A Dirty Job

Florence Nightingale was seven years older than Joseph Lister and already a highly respected nurse when she described an English hospital in 1850: "The nurses did not as a general rule wash patients. The beds on which the patients lay were dirty. It was a common practice to put a new patient into the same sheets used by the last occupant of the bed."[1]

As Joseph studied at medical school and began working in the hospital, he became a first-hand witness to conditions that would horrify any twenty-first century doctor. The environment wasn't unusual to Joseph. But even as a young man, he began to see the effects of such filth, even if he didn't yet understand their link to disease.

As a dresser he wasn't yet qualified to perform surgery. His main role was to be an observer. Here Joseph brought exceptional skills to the job at hand. His artistic ability was used as he drew detailed illustrations of various patients' maladies. The pictures were nearly as good as color photos, something doctors wouldn't have available for several decades.

His compassion as a Quaker also helped. Joseph had to interview patients suffering from gruesome injuries and horrible diseases. His notes seem impartial yet informative.

23

Thanks to his father, Joseph owned the best microscope available, and he used it regularly to examine slides of blood, skin and other matter. His interest in the world invisible to the naked eye would soon serve him well.

Besides his studies, Joseph labored to eliminate his stutter. He joined the debating and medical societies, hoping that public speaking would help overcome the impediment. At the Medical Society, he was elected secretary, then treasurer, and finally in 1852, president.

Illustration of a leg amputation in the 16th century. The surgeon is cutting through the leg with a saw as blood spurts out of the arteries. One of his assistants is collecting the severed limb. The other has temporarily "anesthetised" the patient by hitting him in the head with a padded glove until he lost consciousness. Surgery at this time was painful and risky as anesthetic & antiseptic drugs were not invented until the 19th century. Surgeons simply completed their work as quickly as physically possible. Amputations were often performed to treat gangrene.

He did well in school, earning the prestigious Longridge prize of forty pounds—a considerable amount in 1852. He also qualified as house surgeon. Under the watchful eyes of one of the two surgeons at the hospital, Joseph was able to practice surgery for the first time.

In 1852, Joseph presented one of his first scientific papers to the Medical Society. Few surgeons were as skilled at research as Joseph was, and the papers he presented would earn him a great deal of respect. One of them especially showed the promise of a true scientist. It was about hospital gangrene, a common complication following surgery.

Gangrene occurs when the blood supply to part of the body, usually a limb, is stopped. The affected part turns black, releases pus, and soon begins to smell. If left untreated, it can result in death. The most common way of stopping the disease was to amputate the limb. Sometimes the disease continued to spread after the amputation. No one was sure what caused it.

Working under surgeon John Eric Erichsen, Joseph had stripped off the rotting flesh of a gangrene patient, then tried to heal the wound with acid. His efforts didn't help, and the patient died.

Feeling so helpless must have been discouraging to the young medical student, but it was something every doctor wrestles with eventually. Not every patient can be saved. What would become increasing troubling to Joseph was that many gangrene sufferers survived their operations, only to die in recovery. Joseph knew that he wanted to solve this problem. And he knew that he was destined to be a surgeon.

"If the love of surgery is a proof of a person's being adapted for it, then I am fitted to be a surgeon," he later wrote, "for thou can't hardly conceive what a high degree of enjoyment I am from day to day experiencing in this bloody and butchery department of healing art."[2]

Completing his four-year course load a year early, Joseph earned first honors in an examination on medicine. On December 9, 1852 having passed the required tests, he was a fully qualified surgeon. He spent the early part of 1853 as a house surgeon for the senior hospital physician Walter H. Walshe. On May 4, 1853 he received his Bachelor of Medicine Degree at the University of London.

Once again, Joseph wasn't sure what he wanted to do. He could stay at the University College hospital, develop a private practice, or go elsewhere. In the end, it was the advice of a professor that sent him to Edinburgh, Scotland. It was there that James Syme, the man called "the first of British surgeons," worked. Syme had brought prestige and discipline to a profession once populated by strong and uneducated barbers.

A lawyer's son, Syme put himself through college when his father lost his fortune. Since then he'd done everything from opening a medical school to working as a professor at University College. His time there had been brief, and since it was during Joseph's 1848 breakdown, the two men hadn't met.

Edinburgh was a city of 200,000 and its 200-bed royal infirmary was more than four times as large as the one at University College. Joseph's intention was to study with Syme for a month, then travel to continental Europe to visit other medical schools. Instead, he wouldn't leave Scotland for over thirty years.

The surgeon was so impressed by the papers Joseph wrote that he created a job for him. The position of house surgeon soon came open, and he appointed Joseph over the students he had taught at Edinburgh University. Joseph for his part always admired the older doctor, often telling his students after a surgical demonstration, "Just another of the many things I learned from Mr. Syme."[3]

Joseph began perfecting his surgical technique under Syme's guidance. He also improved his personal life when he met the doctor's older daughter, Agnes.

Joseph and Agnes dated secretly, but by 1854 the relationship was public enough to be parodied in a song performed during a staff dinner.

In the nineteenth century, dating was a very formal affair, but here the traditional Joseph went against tradition. Besides dating Agnes in secret, he waited nearly a year for her father to approve the courtship. He waited even longer to ask him for permission to marry his daughter.

Syme gave Joseph his blessing. Syme treated the young surgeon better than anyone else. They never seemed to argue although Syme had a well-earned reputation for rages. From Syme, Joseph gained confidence, so much so that when he knew he was right he didn't allow other's opinions to affect his feelings.

Agnes and Joseph were married on April 23, 1856. The couple would have a childless marriage. Perhaps the lack of offspring brought the couple closer. They also entered the wedding with a great deal more

Joseph Lister as a young man. This illustration was crafted from a daguerreotype published in London in 1917.

money than most young couples. Between their two fathers, they received over 15,000 pounds in an investment trust, which gave them a steady income.

Agnes's love for Joseph may have come in part because he paid so much attention to her and not her younger sister. Considered to be the plainer of Syme's daughters, Agnes made up for any lack of beauty with a sharp mind and an independent spirit. For the rest of their marriage, Agnes would assist Joseph with his medical experiments and help him with his papers. After years of watching her father's work, Agnes was almost as knowledgeable about medicine as the young medical students who passed through the hospital.

Agnes didn't just alter Joseph's personal life; she affected his religious life as well. Agnes was Episcopalian. She wasn't about to leave her church. Raised as a Quaker, Joseph had been kept away from prestigious Oxford and Cambridge because of his religion. Yet his love for Agnes was sufficient that he agreed to leave his church. An Episcopal minister married them, although the ceremony was held in Syme's home out of respect for Lister's Quaker family.

As his personal life improved, so too did his career. He began teaching classes at Edinburgh and opened a successful private surgical practice. Despite limited spare time, he managed to conduct a wide variety of experiments and publish some fifteen papers in three years detailing the results. It was an incredible output.

In 1859, the Professor of Surgery position at Glasgow University fell vacant. Joseph didn't want to leave Edinburgh, but he knew what a wonderful professional opportunity it was. He applied. Competing against seven applicants, Joseph got official word on January 28, 1860. He had the job.

The next year, he was elected surgeon of the Glasgow Royal Infirmary. Inside the hospital's walls, Joseph would finally explore a way to end hospitalism.

The word "barber" comes from a Latin word that means "beard." For many centuries, trimming beards or shaving men to entirely eliminate facial hair was one of the main responsibilities of barbers.

These responsibilities became enlarged during the Middle Ages. Up to the year 1163, priests and monks had been physicians and surgeons because they were among the few people in that era who were educated. But then the Pope said that clergymen could no longer shed blood. Because barbers were already skilled in using sharp tools on people, they were the logical choice to replace members of religious orders in the practice of surgery. They were soon known as "barber-surgeons" and the phrase "just a little off the top" began to have a whole new meaning.

In some respects, their most important skill was having enough strength to hold down a struggling patient. There were no anesthetics to numb the pain of those unfortunate enough to have an operation performed on them. The distinctive red-and-white striped barber's pole became the profession's symbol.

The pole itself came from a stick that patients would grab to try to ease their pain while the knife cut into them, the red was a reference to their blood and the white represented the bandages that were used to cover their wounds. Barber-surgeons soon formed powerful guilds, similar to modern-day labor unions. That allowed them to carefully regulate the number of members they had.

But surgery began to split off as a separate discipline and surgeons wanted to cease their association with barbers. By 1745, a guild of surgeons separate from the barbers was formed in England. In 1800, the Royal College of Surgeons received its charter and by the mid-1800s surgery was seen as an educated, if low-paying, profession. In the meantime, barbers lost all rights to perform surgery.

French chemist Dr. Louis Pasteur, shown here, was the father of modern bacteriology and pioneer of the treatment of numerous diseases by vaccination.

# 4

# Hospitalism

Before the middle part of the 1800s, surgery was performed without anesthesia. The patient would lie awake in unbearable agony while the surgeon sliced into his flesh. The operations had to be quick. James Syme, Joseph Lister's boss and father-in-law, could cut off a jawbone in less than five minutes. Another doctor not only amputated his patient's leg in less than thirty seconds, he also took his assistant's thumb with it.

Anesthesia changed everything.

The introduction of ether and chloroform enabled more complicated surgeries because the doctor could take his time. Unfortunately, the risk of post-operative infection—called sepsis, ward death, or hospitalism—increased with the number of surgeries. In many hospitals over 40 percent of patients survived amputations only to die during the recovery period.

The battle against sepsis—from the Greek word for rotten—began with Sir John Pringle during the 1750s. An army physician, he noted how wounds became "rotted" and he suggested "anti-septic" to fight the rot.

The question in the 1800s was what to use.

In 1843, a U.S. doctor named Oliver Wendell Holmes wrote an article in the *New England Journal of Medicine*. Holmes said doctors should wash their hands with calcium chloride after treating pregnant women. Hungarian Ignatz Semmelweis went even further. He told the doctors and support staff at his hospital that they should wash their hands in chlorinated lime.

Deaths on the wards Semmelweis ran dropped from 12 percent to one percent. Unfortunately the unpleasantness of the procedure, along with older doctors who were opposed to new ideas, kept it from being used. The Hungarian doctor died in a mental hospital, and few learned about his ideas.

As Joseph Lister settled into his new life in Glasgow he'd never heard of Semmelweis, nor had he read the Holmes article. But he was about to come to his own conclusions about hospitalism. These conclusions would change surgery forever.

Glasgow was a growing city, fed by the migrations of the Industrial Revolution as many people moved from rural farms to urban factories. Because many Glasgow residents were poor or working class, the Glasgow Infirmary provided free medical care. The wealthier could afford private surgeons, and here Joseph made most of his income. Since hospitals didn't provide private rooms for recovery, Joseph would travel to patients' homes or perform surgery at his new residence on 17 Woodside Place.

Between his work at the infirmary and his private practice, Joseph saw patients from all income levels. When he wasn't performing surgery, he was lecturing to his surgical students. Although some saw him as cold, many former students remembered his classes as entertaining. For some reason, the emotionless Lister came alive when demonstrating surgical techniques. Often he told jokes and generally kept his students' attention.

Yet even as he succeeded as a teacher, his experiences as a surgeon deeply affected him. Too many patients were dying.

As the surgeon in charge of the Male Accident Ward, he saw all manner of gruesome injuries. Many required amputation. Keeping careful records, Joseph was shocked to realize that from 1861-1865, nearly half of them died of post-operative sepsis, or hospitalism. Few of his colleagues seemed terribly concerned. This sort of death rate was considered normal.

Others had tried to prevent it. Chemist Justin von Leibig believed it was caused by moist body tissue coming into contact with oxygen. He believed if wounds were covered in plaster or resins, gangrene wouldn't occur.

Though he was wrong, the "bad air" theory held. It was part of the reason why older hospitals were being demolished and new ones were taking their place. Yet the shiny new wing of the Glasgow Infirmary did nothing to drive down the grim mortality statistics.

The puzzle quickly became an obsession for Joseph. For most of the decade, he would only write two papers. Every free moment he spent researching. He explored different methods of operating, wondering if the amputations were responsible, or perhaps the anesthesia. In 1861 he used chloroform on a sheep and began an operation on its larynx, but "I had just got so far with my observations when the inspector of the slaughterhouse walked up and told me he would not allow such brutality," Lister later recalled, " and forthwith ordered me off the premises. Thus, I had a taste of what has been alas! experienced so largely by our profession, how ignorant prejudice with good intentions may obstruct legitimate scientific inquiry."[1]

Joseph was referring to recent animal rights campaigns, which were then sweeping through England. He soon learned that worrying about different operating techniques wasn't going to solve the problem.

His breakthrough didn't come from surgery. It came from sewage.

"In the course of the year 1864," he later wrote in *The Lancet*, "I was much struck with an account of the remarkable effects produced by carbolic acid upon the sewage of the town of Carlisle, the administration of a very small proportion not only preventing all odor from the land irrigated with the refuse material, but as it was stated, destroying the entozoa which usually infect cattle that fed upon such pastures... the applicability of carbolic acid for the treatment of compound fractures naturally occurred to me."[2]

It was his father's pioneering work with the microscope that gave him an understanding of the composition of hospital gangrene, a disease that came most likely from soil bacteria. Indeed, many infections and diseases occur because of bacteria.

As they walked home one chilly Glasgow night, the school's chemistry professor made a recommendation to Joseph. He suggested that he read a series of articles written by a French chemist named Louis Pasteur. Performing experiments with wine fermentation back in the 1850s, Pasteur had noticed that the process that caused wine to ferment was different from that which soured milk. He theorized that this was caused by specific germs—microscopic single-celled organisms called bacteria. Joseph wondered if these same organisms could cause the kinds of gangrene he encountered at the hospital.

By the 1860s, Pasteur's "germ theory of disease" had gained recognition. He believed that germs cause most infectious diseases. His work led to the science of microbiology, the branch of biology dealing with microscopic forms of life.

"Chance favors only the prepared mind," Pasteur once said. And Joseph Lister was well prepared. He began studying ways of combating an organism so small that over a billion could fit in a teaspoon of dirt. A few years later German scientist Robert Koch would develop bacteriology, a new branch of medicine devoted to studying the more than 2,500 different types of these tiny organisms.

Most bacteria are harmless, even helpful. Unfortunately a few can be deadly. One of the more infamous is the *Streptococcus pyogenes* bacteria, which grows in grapelike clumps. Like all bacteria, it reproduces by cell division. This means it splits in half and one cell becomes two. The two soon become four, and so on. Since bacterial cell division can occur every twenty minutes, streptococcus spreads quickly.

Today the bacteria is best known as the cause of strep throat, an infection quite common in children. It is highly contagious and often spreads when an infected person sneezes or coughs. Fortunately, this illness is very treatable today. However, in the nineteenth century infection by the streptococcus was often deadly. Besides the dangers of strep throat, even minor injuries were susceptible to this bacteria. A century ago the tiniest infected cut could be fatal.

Another type of bacteria, *Clostridium Welchii*, was responsible for the gangrene infections that killed so many patients,

By the middle 1860s, Joseph Lister had two ideas spinning in his head:

carbolic acid and germs. They merged into a single thought: antiseptic, a way of preventing sepsis, or hospitalism.

"With regard to the mode in which the atmosphere produces decomposition of the blood," he later wrote in an application to the University of London, "we now know thanks to the beautiful researches of Pasteur, that the active agents are not the gaseous elements of the air, but minute living organisms suspended in it... Hence it occurred to me that if in a compound fracture, before decomposition of the blood has set in, a material were applied to the wound which through it might allow the gases of the atmosphere to penetrate it, would destroy its living germs, all evil consequences might be averted."[3]

Lister didn't get the job at the University of London. But he did have a new way of dealing with hospitalism.

He realized that the best patients to experiment on were those who'd suffered compound fractures, a terrible injury in which the broken bone pierces the skin. These patients often suffered from gangrene and other infections.

By March, 1865, he was able to apply his carbolic theory to two of them. One had a broken wrist, the other a broken leg. Both times he failed. Infection occurred. Amputation was required.

For most of the spring and summer he brooded, considering what he needed to do differently. When eleven-year-old James Greenlees came into the hospital in August, 1865, his leg broken from a collision with a cart, Joseph knew he had to try the technique again. This time, after giving the boy chloroform, he washed the wound completely with a mixture of carbolic acid and linseed oil.

Gangrenous infections have a distinct rotting smell. As Lister examined the boy over the next several days, no such smell was present. There were burns from the acid, but otherwise the wound was healed. His method worked!

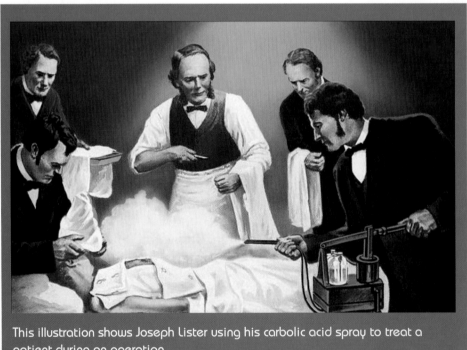

This illustration shows Joseph Lister using his carbolic acid spray to treat a patient during an operation.

*Though animals were used in medical experiments for centuries, the practice didn't become very common until the early part of the nineteenth century. At that point, science began to make rapid advances and the use of animal testing increased as well. It didn't take long for this procedure to face increasingly organized opposition, especially in England.*

*Opponents began forming animal welfare organizations such as the Society for the Prevention of Cruelty to Animals, which was founded in 1824. They drew their arguments from the late eighteenth century philosopher Jeremy Bentham, who felt that experiments that caused an animal to suffer were immoral, and from author Charles Darwin. Darwin's theory of evolution connected human beings to all creatures, but especially to primates like monkeys and chimpanzees that were seen as close relations.*

*Opponents of animal testing in England succeeded in passing a law in 1876 called the Cruelty to Animals Act that restricted the practice. Conducting experiments on living animals, which is called vivisection, had to be approved by the Home Office. The use of cats and dogs in experiments was banned entirely.*

*Joseph Lister fought against these laws, and even argued with Queen Victoria. In 1840, soon after the beginning of her long reign, she had allowed the Society for the Prevention of Cruelty to Animals to add the world "Royal" to its charter. Later she said, "The Queen has done all she could on the dreadful subject of vivisection…a practice which is a disgrace to humanity."[4] When she sent Joseph a letter asking him to support her campaign to end animal testing, he refused. He even added, "An act is cruel or otherwise, not according to the pain which it involves, but according to the mind and object of the actor [the person doing the experiment.]"[5]*

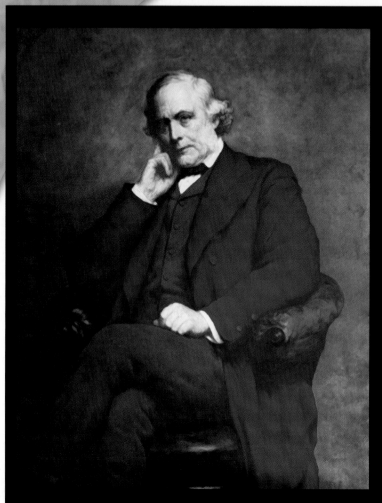

An illustration of Lister from 1895, after the death of his wife. In the same year, Jordan Wheat Lambert began marketing a safer antiseptic that he had discovered in 1879. The product, named Listerine, later became the most widely used mouthwash.

# 5

# A New Era

Joseph Lister had discovered a cure for hospitalism. Now all he had to do was convince everyone else that it worked. Over the next two years, he began doing just that. As head of the accident ward, he had enough authority to see that his methods were put in place. He kept careful records of the results. He watched as the death rates from post-operative infections declined. Yet despite nine months without a single death from sepsis, there were still skeptics. In one hospital, they'd joke, "Shut the door quickly or one of Mr. Lister's microbes will come in."

In March 1867, Joseph Lister published the results of his work in *The Lancet*. After detailing his work, and showing how it applied not just to compound fractures but also to a whole variety of injuries, he concluded by saying "Since the antiseptic treatment has been brought into full operation, and wounds and abscess no longer poison the atmosphere with putrid exhalations, my wards, though in other respects under precisely the same circumstances as before, have completely changed their character."[1] As he noted that not a single case of gangrene had occurred the previous year, he presented his findings to the medical community.

The response was immediate.

"If Professor Lister's conclusions with regard to the power of carbolic acid in compound fractures should be confirmed by further experimentation and observation," an editorial in the August issue of *The Lancet* proclaimed, "it will be difficult to overrate the importance of what we may really call his discovery."

Not everyone agreed. Hospitals in England and France were less interested in the technique. On a tour of the United States, Lister only convinced doctors in New York and Boston. Yet the truth of his methods was demonstrated by their success. Wherever his techniques were implemented, lives were saved.

The most dramatic example occurred during a war. In battle shrapnel— very hot metal from exploding bombs and bullets—often drives bacteria deep into a wound. Gangrene results. This type of bacterial infection was the most difficult to treat, and even Lister's methods didn't eliminate it. But during the Franco-Prussian War in 1870, German doctors using the technique saved the lives of thousands of their soldiers. A few years later, another German named Robert Koch began using steam to sterilize surgical instruments. That made operations even safer.

By the time Joseph began as a professor of surgery at Kings College in London, he was able to persuade the doubters who'd harshly judged his technique merely because it had been developed in Scotland. His job put him at the forefront of surgical teaching. It was considered one of the most respected posts in the world. By now he'd educated an entire generation of surgeons and they were quick to embrace new methods of antiseptics.

The success of his method also expanded the possibility of operations. When his sister Isabella contracted breast cancer, Joseph himself performed the operation. Although it didn't eliminate the cancer, she lived for three years afterward, longer than she would have survived without the surgery. He even performed surgery on Queen Victoria and became her official surgeon.

By 1890, the death rate from major operations had declined to 7.1 percent. The doubters had been eliminated by the statistics. By the time of his seventy-seventh birthday, the *Daily Chronicle* newspaper pointed out the obvious: "But for the antiseptic surgery of which he is the founder, a multitude of men alive today would be dead or maimed...Lord Lister has made, on a large scale, our English manhood whole."

Joseph's life as a surgeon and researcher ended with his wife's death in 1892. Although he was honored with several royal titles and appointed President of the Royal Society, he became a recluse, retiring to his estate in Walmer in Kent County. Blind and almost completely deaf, Lister died on February 10, 1912. But because of his efforts, surgeons became far more careful about germs, and began wearing sterile operating gowns, masks, and eventually gloves.

Joseph's name also lives on in a common household product. In 1879, Dr. Joseph Lawrence discovered a new antiseptic that was safer than carbolic acid. He named his invention to honor Joseph and then sold the rights to Jordan Wheat Lambert, who soon began to market the new product. It didn't take long to realize that it also killed germs in peoples' mouths, so in 1895 Lambert started selling it to dentists. Within 20 years it became the most widely used mouthwash in the world. It is, of course, Listerine.

Family values, a strong work ethic, thrift, religion: all of these qualities were a significant part of the Lister household. They were also the cornerstones of the Victorian era. The period got its name from Queen Victoria, who was born in 1819. She became queen in 1837 at the age of 18. In 1840, she married her cousin Albert, a German prince. They would have nine children during the next thirteen years.

The values of her country were inspired by her rule. By the late 1800s, England was at the peak its power. There was a saying that "the sun never sets on the British Empire." That was because nearly one fourth of the earth's surface was under the control of Great Britain.

Queen Victoria influenced her country medically as well. One of her most famous acts was using chloroform, a type of anesthetic, during the births of her final two children. Up to that time, many doctors and other people had serious reservations about using anesthetics to help in childbirth. After the queen's successful experiences, many of her countrywomen were willing to use anesthetics. Victoria also supported Joseph Lister, who was controversial for his promotion of antiseptics.

Queen Victoria

Yet for all its advances, the rigid, prudish life of Victorian England quickly fell out of favor with the dawn of the twentieth century. In many ways the end of the Victorian era was marked not just by the end of the 1800s but also by the death of its namesake leader in 1901 after more than 63 years on the throne. As Joseph Lister later said, "What a terrible blow the Queen's death was. Yet it seemed to come about at the right time."[2]

# Chronology

| | |
|---|---|
| **1827** | Born on April 5 in Upton Park, Essex, England |
| **1838** | Begins attending Hitchin School in Hertfordshire |
| **1841** | Begins attending Grove House in Tattenham |
| **1843** | Enrolls at University College, taking a botany course |
| **1845** | Accepted as a full time student at University College |
| **1847** | Graduates from University College with a Bachelor of Arts degree |
| **1848** | Suffers from depression, travels and recovers |
| **1849** | Registers as medical student at University College |
| **1852** | Passes exams allowing him to work as a surgeon |
| **1853** | Receives Bachelor of Medicine degree; moves to Edinburgh, Scotland |
| **1856** | Marries Agnes Syme on April 23 |
| **1860** | Becomes professor of surgery at Glasgow University |
| **1865** | First applies antiseptic principle to wounds |
| **1867** | Publishes papers in *The Lancet* detailing discovery of antiseptic principles |
| **1869** | Is appointed professor of surgery at Edinburgh |
| **1877** | Accepts position as Professor of Surgery at Kings College, London |
| **1892** | Agnes dies |
| **1895** | Becomes President of Royal Society |
| **1897** | Made Baron Lister of Lyme Regis |
| **1902** | Appointed member of Order of Merit |
| **1912** | Dies on February 10 in Walmer, Kent |

# Timeline of Discovery

| | |
|---|---|
| **500 B.C.** | Descriptions of using fungi and molds to fight skin infections appear in Egypt. |
| **1752** | Sir John Pringle publishes *Observations on the Diseases of the Army*, which notes how battle injuries become "rotted," and proposes use of good sanitation and well-ventilated barracks. |
| **1796** | English doctor Edward Jenner conducts the first vaccination with cowpox to create immunity to smallpox, at that time one of the leading causes of death. |
| **1824** | Joseph Jackson Lister begins his work on microscope lenses. |
| **1843** | U.S. physician Oliver Wendell Holmes writes in the *New England Journal of Medicine* that physicians should wash their hands in calcium chloride after treating pregnant women. |
| **1848** | Hungarian doctor Ignatz Semmelweis advises everyone who examines patients to rinse their hands in chlorinated lime. |
| **1865** | Louis Pasteur begins research on his theory that specific diseases are caused by specific bacteria. |
| **1870-71** | A dramatic decline in infections during the Franco-Prussian war among wounded soldiers following surgery is credited to Lister's call for clean operating rooms and the use of diluted carbolic acid. |
| **1870s/80s** | German doctor Robert Koch's work leads to the creation of bacteriology, the study of bacteria. |
| **1875** | John Tyndall notes the bacteria-fighting ability of "Penicilliums," part of the fungi family which also includes mushrooms and mold. |
| **1879** | Dr. Joseph Lawrence invents Listerine. |
| **1884** | Russian-French bacteriologist Elie Metchknikoff observes white blood cells' ability to fight infection. |
| **1890** | American physician William Halsted invents surgical gloves. |
| **1919** | Mercurochrome, an antiseptic applied to the skin to prevent infection, is introduced. |
| **1920** | Earle Dickson, an employee of Johnson & Johnson, invents the Band-Aid. |
| **1928** | Scottish scientist Alexander Fleming discovers penicillin. |
| **1940s** | Penicillin becomes widely available for treating infections. |
| **1955** | Dr. Jonas Salk announces the discovery of polio vaccine. |
| **1992** | Listerine Cool Mint is introduced to appeal to younger people. |
| **2003** | New techniques such as administering antibiotics one hour prior to surgery and clipping instead of shaving body hair reduce risk of post-operative infection. |

# Chapter Notes

### Chapter One: Cause of Death

1. Joseph Lister, "Antiseptic Principle of the Practice of Surgery," *The Lancet,* December 16, 1867, (Internet Source Book), p. 123.

2. Charles Dickens, *A Christmas Carol and Other Christmas Stories,* (New York: Penguin, 1984), Chapter 4.

3. *The Lancet,* December 1869.

### Chapter Two: Friendly Persuasions

1. Joseph Lister, "Antiseptic Principle of the Practice of Surgery," *The Lancet,* December 16, 1867, (Internet Source Book), p. 27.

2. Ibid., p. 28.

3. Ibid., p. 38.

4. Ibid., p. 42.

5. Ibid., p. 43.

6. http://www.pendle.net/Attractions/quakers.htm.

### Chapter Three: A Dirty Job

1. Cecil Woodham-Smith, *Florence Nightingale 1820-1910,* (London: Constable, 1950), p. 128.

2. Joseph Lister, "Antiseptic Principle of the Practice of Surgery," *The Lancet,* December 16, 1867, (Internet Source Book), p. 47.

3. Ibid., p. 60.

### Chapter Four: Hospitalism

1. Joseph Lister, "Antiseptic Principle of the Practice of Surgery," *The Lancet,* December 16, 1867, (Internet Source Book), p. 218.

2. *The Lancet,* December 1869.

3. Lister, 140.

4. http://www.ivu.org/people/quotes/experim.html.

5. Lister, 218.

### Chapter Five: A New Era

1. *The Lancet,* March 16, 1867.

2. Joseph Lister, "Antiseptic Principle of the Practice of Surgery," *The Lancet,* December 16, 1867, (Internet Source Book), p. 311.

# Glossary

**anesthesia**   (ann-is-THEE-zha) - chemical which produces unconscious state in patients

**antibiotic**   (ann-tih-by-OUGHT-ick) - a natural substance which destroys germs

**antiseptic**   (ann-tih-SEP-tick) - a chemical substance which destroys germs

**bacteria**   (back-TEAR-ee-uh) - microscopic single-celled organisms; some are dangerous, some are helpful, most are harmless

**bacteriologist**   (back-TEAR-ee-all-oh-jist) - scientist who studies bacteria and looks for ways to fight diseases they cause

**infection**   (in-FECK-shun) - disease caused by germs

**strain**   particular variety or group of microbes

# For Further Reading

**Works Consulted:**

Anderson, Eric. "Here's to the Giants of Medicine," *Medical Economics,* Dec. 20 1999, p. 64.

Dickens, Charles. *A Christmas Carol and Other Christmas Stories.* New York: Penguin, 1984 (1843).

Fisher, Richard B. *Joseph Lister.* New York: Stein and Day, 1977.

Kandela, Peter. "Antisepsis." *The Lancet,* March 13, 1999, p. 937.

Lister, Joseph. "Antiseptic Principle of the Practice of Surgery," *The Lancet,* Dec.16, 1867 (Internet Source Book) also Aug. 24, and March16, 1867.

Woodham-Smith, Cecil. *Florence Nightingale 1820-1910.* London: Constable, 1950.

**For Young Adults:**

DeJauregui, Ruth. *100 Medical Milestones.* San Mateo, California: Bluebird Books, 1998.

McTavish, Douglas. *Joseph Lister.* New York: Franklin Watts 1992.

**On the Web:**

A Brief History of Lab Animal Use
http://www.hsus.org/ace/11390

"Antiseptic Principle Of The Practice Of Surgery, 1867": Joseph Lister (1827-1912)
http://www.fordham.edu/halsall/mod/1867lister.html

Gallery Guide - Joseph Jackson Lister's microscope (1826)
http://www.sciencemuseum.org.uk/galleryguide/E5281.asp

Joseph Lister
http://www.historylearningsite.co.uk/joseph_lister.htm

Joseph Lister and Antiseptic Surgery
http://web.ukonline.co.uk/b.gardner/Lister.html

Quakers and Pendle
http://www.pendle.net/Attractions/quakers.htm

SJSU Virtual Museum
http://www.sjsu.edu/depts/Museum/lis.html

Victorian Britain
http://learningcurve.pro.gov.uk/victorianbritain/default.htm

# Index

48